Contents

Some words are shown in bold, **like this**.
They are explained in the glossary on page 23.

What are bicycles?

Bicycles are **vehicles** with two wheels.

Bicycles can carry people and things.

brake

pedal

wheel

People push pedals to make the wheels turn round.

They use brakes to stop.

What do bicycles look like?

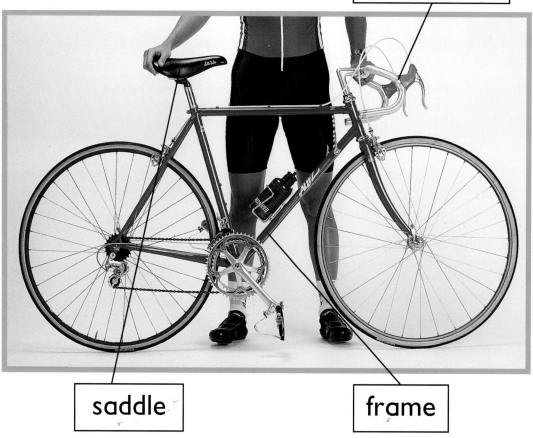

handlebars

saddle

frame

Bicycles have a **frame** to hold the wheels together.

Bicycles have **handlebars** and a saddle.

Bicycles are also called bikes.

They come in many colours.

What are bicycles made of?

frame

pedal

Bicycle **frames** are made of metal.

Some pedals are made of metal and rubber.

saddle handgrips tyre

Tyres and handgrips are made of rubber.

Bicycle saddles are made of plastic.

How did bicycles look in the past?

The first bicycle was made of wood.

It had no pedals. People pushed it along with their feet.

Later, bicycles had pedals.

They had big front wheels and tiny back wheels.

What is a BMX bicycle?

BMX bicycles are small and light.

People can do tricks on them.

Some people race BMX bikes on muddy tracks.

They wear a special **helmet** in case they fall off.

What is a racing bicycle?

Racing bicycles are very light.

They go fast in races.

Riders lean down over the **handlebars**.

They have to push the pedals hard to go fast.

What is a track bicycle?

Track bicycles and racing bicycles look the same.

But track bicycles do not have brakes.

People ride track bicycles in
a **velodrome**.

This is a special racing track
with steep sides.

What is a mountain bike?

tyre

Mountain bikes have thick, bumpy **tyres**.

These can roll over sticks and rocks.

People ride mountain bikes on trails.

Some people ride mountain bikes
up hills.

Why are some bicycles special?

Tandems are bicycles for two people.

They have two saddles and two sets of pedals.

Pedicabs have three wheels.

They have extra seats
for **passengers**.

Bicycle map

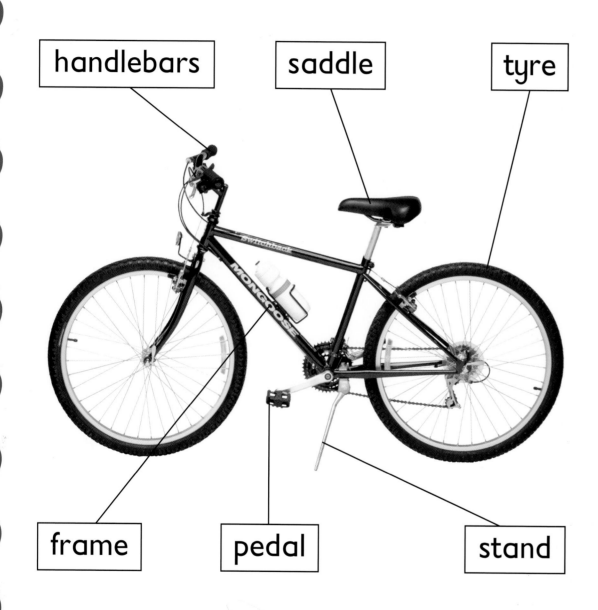

handlebars

saddle

tyre

frame

pedal

stand

Glossary

frame
triangle-shaped piece of metal that holds the parts of a bicycle together

handlebars
steering part of a bicycle or another vehicle

helmet
special hard hat that bicycle riders must wear to protect their heads

passenger
person who rides on a vehicle that somebody else is driving

tyre
rubber strip on the outside of a wheel to give a smooth ride

vehicle
machine that carries people and things from place to place

velodrome
racing track with steep sides, for track bikes to race on

Index

24

Titles in the Wheels, Wings and Water series include:

Hardback   1 844 21371 4

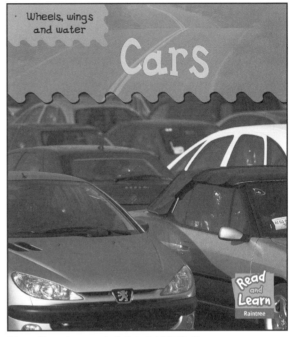

Hardback   1 844 21372 2

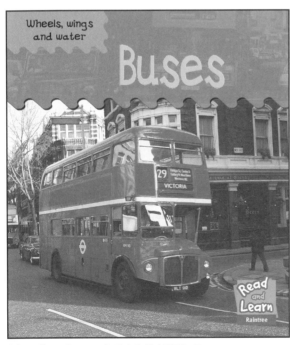

Hardback   1 844 21373 0

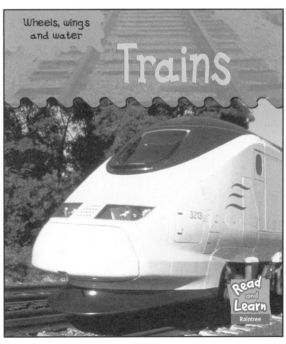

Hardback   1 844 21374 9

Find out about the other titles in this series on our website www.raintreepublishers.co.uk